OTHER BIOGRAPHIES AVAILABLE IN YEARLING BOOKS:

Duke Ellington

KING OF JAZZ

by Elizabeth Rider Montgomery

illustrated by Paul Frame

A YEARLING BOOK

For Linda Phillips

Published by
Dell Publishing Co., Inc.
1 Dag Hammarskjold Plaza
New York, New York 10017

PICTURE CREDITS:
Brown Brothers: p. 54
Culver Pictures: p. 71
Schomburg Collection, New York Public Library: p. 38
United Press International: p. 90
Wide World Photos: p. 93

DUKE ELLINGTON is one of the Americans All biographies
published by Garrard Publishing Company, Champaign, Illinois.
Americans All books are published by Garrard in library bindings.

Contents

1. No Thrill in Piano Practice

Eight-year-old Edward Ellington sat on the piano stool in the parlor. Dutifully he fingered the scales he had been told to practice. However, his eyes kept straying toward the open window. He could hear, faintly, the shouts of his friends. They were playing baseball in the vacant lot behind the YMCA building, several blocks away.

Suddenly Edward heard someone running up the steps of his home. The front door burst open, and a girl's voice called out, "Aunt Daisy! Can Edward come out and play?" It was one of his cousins. Dozens of cousins of various ages lived nearby. They were always running in and out of the Ellington house.

Edward's fingers were idle on the piano keys as he listened to his mother's reply. She told his cousin he could not play. He had to practice for the concert to be given at the church the following week.

Edward sighed. He began the A scale again. How he hated piano practice! He had been taking music lessons less than a year, but it seemed forever. If he could work on tunes like "The Rosary," music might be fun. His mother played that piece beautifully. But who wanted to practice scales and exercises? And who wanted to study dull pieces like the one his teacher said he had to play at the church concert?

Again the house became quiet. Edward continued practicing. Suddenly he heard a whisper. It came from the open window.

"Hey, Edward!"

Silently Edward slipped from the piano stool over to the window. One of his friends stood there, waving his baseball glove. He told Edward the baseball team needed him at second base.

Edward glanced at the hall door, then he put one leg over the windowsill. Ten seconds later he was racing with his friend toward their ball field.

His mother would soon miss him, of course. She would call and call. When his father came home from work, he would search for him. But by then the ball game should be over.

It was the year 1907, in Washington, D.C. The Ellingtons lived in an all-black section of the city. When Edward was little, his father had been a butler at the White House. Now Mr. Ellington was a blueprint maker for the United States Navy.

Mr. Ellington was friendly and easygoing. He never worried about anything. Mrs. Ellington, on the other hand, was serious, quiet, and deeply religious. She taught Edward to say his prayers and to read the Bible every day. The Ellingtons adored Edward, their only child, and gave him his way in nearly everything.

Yet they insisted on piano lessons. Both parents played the piano, and they both believed their son had musical talent. They intended to give him a good musical education.

This was not the only time Edward played hookey from piano practice. Nevertheless, his performance at the church concert went off well. Both Mr. and Mrs. Ellington beamed with pride. Even Edward's music teacher was pleased.

2. "You'll Never Amount to Anything"

Piano practice was always a dull chore for Edward, but he was not allowed to stop taking lessons. When he entered Armstrong High School in February 1914, he attended classes in music. He also kept on with private lessons.

Everybody called him "Duke" now, because of his princely bearing, his neat clothes, and his charming manners. Duke was more interested in drawing and painting than in any of the other subjects he studied at high school. He especially enjoyed painting posters and signs. But music attracted him too, in spite of his dislike of lessons.

Several of Duke's friends played instruments. Edna Thompson, a neighbor, played the piano quite well. Another neighbor, Otto Hardwicke, studied bass fiddle. A school friend, Arthur Whetsol, played cornet. Soon music became about the most important thing in Duke's life. He began to spend most of his spare time at the piano, playing ragtime.

In ragtime music, the left hand keeps up a strict two-four beat. However, the melody is syncopated; that is, the accent does not fall on the first beat of a measure, as is usually the case. Instead, the weak after-beat is accented. Ragtime is loud, exciting music. Duke liked it.

One day Duke sat at his desk in a class at school. The teacher was explaining

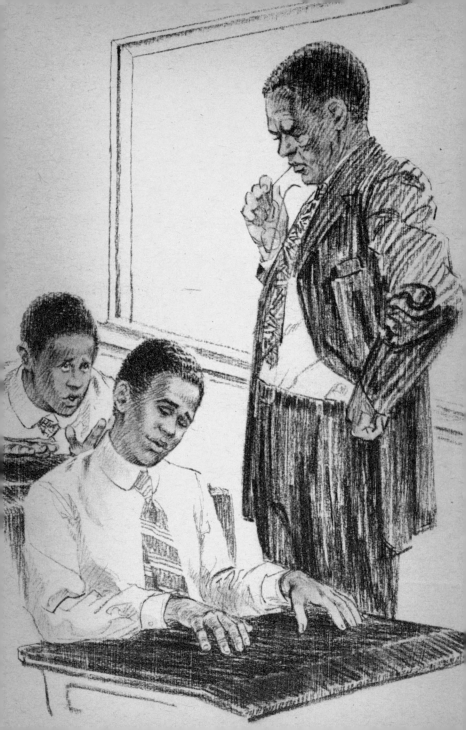

something important, but Duke was not listening. His eyes were almost closed. He ran his fingers back and forth on his desk, "playing" a tune that was running through his head. Behind Duke, Arthur Whetsol began to beat out the rhythm on his own desk.

The teacher stopped in the middle of a sentence. He glared at Duke and scolded him for not paying attention.

Duke dropped his hands in his lap. He turned on the bright smile that never failed to get him his way with parents, aunts, uncles, and friends. But the charming smile had absolutely no effect on his angry teacher.

"You're never going to amount to anything, Ellington!" Duke's instructor said crossly. "Never!"

Duke was sorry he had angered his

teacher, but his devotion to music remained unchanged.

Duke and his friends had begun to attend parties where each one paid a small sum to hear expert pianists play ragtime.

One pianist at these parties threw his hands in the air from time to time while playing. Duke thought this was very flashy, and he learned how to do it too.

Then Duke thought he would try to compose some ragtime music himself. He decided to take lessons in composition and harmony.

Mr. and Mrs. Ellington heard their son at the piano hour after hour. They must have smiled at each other sometimes. If they were sorry that he seemed more interested in ragtime than in classical music, they never said anything.

3. "Soda Fountain Rag"

James P. Johnson was one of the most popular ragtime pianists of the day. Duke admired him and decided to study his music.

At the beginning of summer vacation in 1914, Duke bought a player-piano roll of Johnson's "Carolina Shout." He put the roll on the Ellingtons' upright piano, which had a player attachment. When the switch was turned on, the network of holes in the player roll guided the piano's works. The keys were depressed as if by

A few weeks later Duke got a job at the soda fountain in the Poodle Dog Café. It was near the Washington Senators' ball park. Duke decided to name his ragtime composition "Soda Fountain Rag."

In the following weeks Duke played his "Soda Fountain Rag" many times for small groups of friends and relatives. However, he longed for a chance to play it in public.

One summer evening the pianist at the Poodle Dog Café failed to show up. The manager was worried. People who came to the café expected music, and he had no one to play for them.

When Duke learned this, he hurried to the manager and offered to play the piano. The manager looked doubtfully at the slender, handsome youth.

"Can you entertain people all evening?"

he asked. "Do you know enough different pieces to do that?"

Duke gulped. The only pieces he knew by heart were Johnson's "Carolina Shout" and his own "Soda Fountain Rag." However, he assured the café manager that he knew lots of music.

The manager looked doubtful, but he was desperate. He gave his permission, and Duke hurried over to the piano. He started a spirited performance of "Soda Fountain Rag."

The diners clapped. Duke smiled at them gratefully. Next he played "Carolina Shout" and received more applause.

Then he sat on the piano stool and looked around the café. The manager stood across the room, waving to him to continue. Duke wondered what to do next.

Then he had an idea. He would play

"Soda Fountain Rag" in many different ways. He would play it in waltz time; he would play it as a lively march and as a dreamy ballad; he would play it as a one-step, as a two-step, and as a fox-trot.

When the evening ended, the manager complimented his young pianist.

"You were great," he told the exhausted boy. No one had recognized "Soda Fountain Rag" in its many different forms!

4. Advertising Pays

Duke had a problem. He could not decide whether to make a career of art or music. He did very well in ˙his drawing classes. When the National Association for the Advancement of Colored People held a poster contest, Duke entered it and won. His art teachers hoped he would keep on with drawing and painting.

However, music also fascinated Duke Ellington. During his senior year in high school, he formed a small "combo," with

Otto Hardwicke, Arthur Whetsol, and sometimes other friends. Whetsol played cornet and, later, the trumpet. Hardwicke soon changed from the bass fiddle to the saxophone.

Duke's combo got a few jobs playing at dances and cafés. They called themselves "The Washingtonians." They played jazz, which was new then.

Jazz had grown out of ragtime. African tribal music, slave work songs, spirituals, and "blues" had contributed to jazz. So had European classical music and various dance forms. Jazz is lively music with complex rhythms. Years later Duke described it as "music with an African foundation, which came out of an American environment."

One spring day in 1917, Duke came home from school with some news. He

Now that he had settled on a musical career, Duke began to make plans. The first step toward a successful career was to make his band as well known as possible. Duke had noticed that the most popular bands in Washington, D.C., were advertised in the telephone directory. So he decided to have a bigger ad than anybody else. He told the printer to set his name in large type. He wanted it to stand out more than any other band leader's.

The ad got results. Soon the Washingtonians were offered more engagements than they could handle. Duke turned the extra jobs over to other bands. In a few months he was playing piano for his own combo nearly every night. He was also managing five other bands.

5. Music or Art?

In 1918, at the age of nineteen, Duke married Edna Thompson, a girl in his neighborhood. They had been friends for years. The young couple moved into an apartment of their own, not far from Duke's parents.

Duke's income was growing fantastically. However, he spent the money as fast as it came in. He loved to buy things for his family—his wife, his parents, and his little sister. His sister had been born when he was sixteen.

Duke soon realized that the struggle between art and music had not yet been really settled. Although his evenings were devoted to piano playing, he had time during the day for painting and drawing. Duke enjoyed painting signs. With a friend he started a sign-painting business.

Duke also enjoyed drawing. After his son Mercer was born in 1919, Duke often sketched his wife and baby. He must have thought at times that he would not have to choose between music and art after all.

However, music demanded more and more of his time. Duke had to arrange jobs for all his bands and play the piano for the Washingtonians half the night. How could he paint all day too? He had to have time to sleep and eat.

How Duke loved to eat! After playing all evening, the musicians would go to a café. Before touching a bite, Duke always bowed his head for a silent prayer, as his mother had taught him. Then he might eat two steaks covered with onions, a double helping of fried potatoes, and a big salad with lots of sliced tomatoes. He usually had a gigantic, specially ordered "Ellington dessert." This was an incredible combination of various sweets. It might include cake, custard, pie, jello, fruit, *and* ice cream! Duke's appetite was the marvel of his band.

One evening Duke and his Washingtonians went to the Howard Theater to hear a well-known orchestra from New York. Otto Hardwicke had made friends with the drummer, Sonny Greer. He told Duke that Sonny was really "fly."

Sonny's performance convinced Duke that Hardwicke was right. At the end of the concert, Duke, Hardwicke, and Whetsol waited on the street corner. Soon the flashy drummer came out of the theater. Duke, looking very stylish in his new plaid suit, stopped the New Yorker. He invited him to a jam session. A jam session is a meeting of jazz musicians to play for their own enjoyment. Often the music is created on the spot.

Sonny agreed, and the group went to Duke's house with their instruments. Duke sat down at the piano and began to play. Sonny Greer accented the rhythm on the drums. Soon Otto Hardwicke played his own version of the theme on his saxophone, accompanied by all the others. Then Arthur Whetsol took up the theme on his trumpet and invented another variation, or different way of playing Duke's tune.

Then Duke took a turn. He began to play the theme in yet another way. The piano keys danced under his nimble fingers as he changed the rhythm and added notes for a new variation.

Suddenly, with a lift of his eyebrows, Duke gave the solo spot to Sonny. The little drummer went into action. At first the others were so fascinated by the acrobatics of the drumsticks that they forgot their own instruments. But soon all four were playing together, making loud, harmonious, and exciting music.

The jam session did not end until early in the morning. By this time, Sonny was impressed with Duke Ellington and his Washingtonians. He agreed to join them.

Duke was jubilant. Now they had a real professional in their band.

The busy, happy months flew past. The

Washingtonians became more and more popular in the city from which they drew their name, and Duke and his men were living high.

One night in 1922 Sonny Greer showed up for a rehearsal waving a telegram. The band was going to New York, he said.

The others crowded around Sonny to read the telegram. It was from a New York band leader, Wilbur Sweatman. He wanted Sonny to join his group in New York City. However, Sonny refused to go without Otto Hardwicke and Duke. Arthur Whetsol had recently left the band to continue his medical training.

A few days later Duke, Sonny, and Otto boarded a train for New York. They were full of hope and confidence. Duke's wife and three-year-old son would remain in Washington until he sent for them.

6. One Hot Dog for Five

Duke found New York City busy, noisy, and exciting. He wanted to see it all at once, but Sonny took his friends directly to Harlem.

Harlem was the part of New York City where most blacks lived. It was like a city in itself, with stores, churches, schools, and nightclubs. The finest black writers and poets were gathered there. Among these men were W.E.B. Du Bois, Countee Cullen, and Langston Hughes. Duke may have met some of them, as well as the

Duke and his friends enjoyed living in Harlem (above), the gathering place for black writers, athletes, and musicians.

famous sports champions and popular entertainers of the day.

The greatest black musicians lived in Harlem too. Late at night, when the Washingtonians had finished playing in Sweatman's band, they went on to lively parties. Often they visited nightclubs too. Sonny Greer got them past the doorman without paying.

"Meet my pals, Duke and Otto," he would say. "Duke plays a whole lot of piano." The doorman always let them in free.

In Harlem Duke heard the nation's top jazz players, including James P. Johnson, the composer of "Carolina Shout." Duke became friendly with Johnson's brilliant young pupil, the piano player Fats Waller. Duke and Fats often took turns playing the piano in jam sessions.

The Sweatman engagement did not last long. Soon Duke and his friends were tramping the streets of Harlem, looking for another job. Their money ran low, and they grew very hungry. Duke often thought longingly of the huge meals he used to eat back home in Washington. Memories of the hot biscuits and the delicious fried chicken his mother cooked made his mouth water. Yet he hated to give up and go home a failure. Besides, he realized now that New York was important to a musical career.

One day Duke was walking aimlessly along Lenox Avenue in Harlem. He had been in New York three months. He no longer looked elegant and confident. His shoes were literally falling apart from his daily search for work.

Duke was ready at last to return to

Washington, D.C. However, he had no money for train fare. He had always spent his income without thought of saving.

Suddenly something white caught his eye. An envelope lay on the sidewalk. Duke's sense of neatness made him stop and pick it up.

There was something inside the envelope. He opened it and found $15 in bills! Without delay, Duke bought three railroad tickets to Washington for Sonny Greer, Otto Hardwicke, and himself.

Back home again, Duke tried to take up where he had left off with his sign painting and his band work. However, he knew that this life in Washington was only temporary. If he was to become famous as a musician, he must move to New York.

The following spring Fats Waller came to Washington, playing in a road show. He urged Duke to return to New York. But Duke did not want to go unless he was sure of a job.

A few weeks later Duke got a telegram telling of a job opening in a New York nightclub. Once again the Washingtonians took a train to the big city. Now there were five of them: Duke, Otto Hardwicke, Sonny Greer, Arthur Whetsol, who had again left school, and a newcomer, Elmer Snowden, who played the banjo.

When Duke's Washingtonians arrived at the nightclub, they found that there was no job waiting after all.

"I have all the entertainers I need right now," the nightclub manager told Duke. "Come back next week, and I'll have a place for you."

The Washingtonians returned the following week, but again the manager shook his head. "I'm sorry," he said. "No room yet. Come back next week."

Week after week it was the same story. Duke and his friends again ran out of money. Once they pooled their few coins to buy a single hot dog, which they split five ways. Duke must have wondered if he would have to return to Washington a failure once more.

7. "Ellington, Inc."

After five discouraging weeks, Duke's Washingtonians got a break. They landed a job at Barron's, a high-class nightclub in Harlem. Duke's wife left four-year-old Mercer in Washington, D.C., with his grandmother and joined her husband in New York City.

Soon Elmer Snowden left the Washingtonians, and Freddie Guy joined as a banjoist. From the piano, Duke directed the band. He used his head, his eyebrows, his shoulders, and his hands to signal changes of tempo, mood, and volume. He also gave a nod to tell each man when to take a solo.

In September 1923, after six successful months at Barron's, the Washingtonians got a still better engagement. They went to the Hollywood Café, later called the Kentucky Club. Duke's reputation as a band leader grew steadily, and the Kentucky Club drew large crowds.

Again Arthur Whetsol left the band to return to his medical studies. Duke got Bubber Miley to take his place.

Bubber played the trumpet like nobody else. He was among the first to use a mute, a cuplike rubber device. By pulling the mute to and from his trumpet, Bubber could make his instrument snarl, growl, whine, wail, sob, laugh, and sing. It could almost speak!

Bubber Miley's "talking trumpet" inspired Duke to compose music for him. Duke and Bubber between them worked out "East St. Louis Toodle-oo." This became the theme song of the Washingtonians.

Duke felt the need for more knowledge about music composition. Will M. Cook, a good friend and great violinist, agreed to teach him.

Duke hired a taxi, and the two men rode around Central Park hour after hour while Cook gave lectures on music. Duke would sing a melody, and then Cook would analyze it. He would tell Duke what could be done with his theme. In Duke's opinion, these taxi lectures were the equal of a full course in music theory at a school of music.

During his stay at the Kentucky Club, Duke wrote "Creole Love Call," "Jubilee Stomp," and "Black and Tan Fantasy," as well as "East St. Louis Toodle-oo."

In his compositions, Duke tried to capture the special qualities of the American blacks. He pictured their love of music and their deep spiritual beliefs. He put in their bitterness at years of oppression and their long, heartbreaking struggle for equality.

Duke's music was seldom played exactly as he wrote it. During rehearsals the musicians expressed their feeling about a piece on their instruments. Otto Hardwicke's saxophone might sing one variation of Duke's theme, while Bubber's trumpet growled a different one. Duke might nod approvingly at Otto and shake his head at Bubber, or the other way

around. Sonny Greer might have some new ideas about rhythm, or Freddie Guy about harmony. By the time the music was ready for performance, each member of the band had set his mark on it.

When Duke Ellington and his band had been at the Kentucky Club for three and a half years, Irving Mills dropped in one night to hear them. Mills was a well-known musicians' agent, song publisher, and lyric writer.

Mills sat at a table with a newswriter friend, listening to the music. He was especially struck by the unusual rhythm and distinctive harmony in one number. He went up to the platform and asked Duke the name of the piece.

" 'St. Louis Blues,' " Duke answered.

Mills raised his eyebrows. "It sure didn't sound like 'St. Louis Blues,' " he said.

Later in the evening the band played Duke's "Black and Tan Fantasy." Mills was even more impressed. He recognized that he had met a great creative artist. Duke, he felt, was the first American composer to catch in his music the true jazz spirit.

A few days later Mills approached Duke with a contract offer. He and Duke would form a company, to be called "Ellington, Inc." Mills would be Duke's agent and lyric writer. He would handle all business details and publicity, and Duke would be free to concentrate on his music. Ellington and Mills would share equally in the money the band earned, and Duke would be given a share of some other Mills' properties. Mills promised to make Duke Ellington famous all over the world. Duke signed the contract.

Irving Mills kept his word. He set up recording sessions for the band. He got engagements for them at theaters and at ballrooms. Under Mills' management the band was enlarged to ten. Among the new members was seventeen-year-old Harry Carney, baritone saxophonist.

In December 1927, Mills booked Duke Ellington and his orchestra at Harlem's famous Cotton Club. Johnny Hodges, saxophonist, joined at this time, and Arthur Whetsol returned. Duke's band was now one of New York's largest.

Duke lived in style in a large apartment. He hired a valet, whom he called "Jonesy." Now that he could afford fashionable clothing, Duke had a large wardrobe. He looked more than ever like a duke.

8. Ups and Downs

Duke Ellington had come to be known as one of the best composers and band leaders in the country. Other composers tried to copy his style and his music. However, no one really could, because both his style and his music were too distinctive to be copied.

In 1929 Bubber Miley decided to leave the band. Duke brought in Cootie Williams to replace him. Cootie soon learned how to use a mute. In time, he even improved on Bubber's technique.

Irving Mills continued to keep the band busy, especially with recording sessions. He got them a contract to make a movie, *Check and Double-Check*, with "Amos 'n' Andy," who were popular radio characters of the day. He sent the band on a tour through middle-western America and the West Coast states.

It was a relief to Duke to be free from business worries about his band. Now he had more time for his family. His parents moved from Washington to New York. His sixteen-year-old sister Ruth and his twelve-year-old son Mercer came with them. The whole family lived together in a fine apartment overlooking the Harlem River.

In 1933 Irving Mills arranged a trip to Europe for the band. Duke was pleased with the reception he was given there. In

Duke directs his big band in a lively jazz
number at a show in the 1930s.

America he was called a "jazz writer,"
but in Europe he was considered a serious
composer. London music critics compared
his music with that of Delius and Ravel.
His working methods were likened to
those of Bach, Haydn, and Mozart. Like
these three classical composers, Duke
wrote a lot of music. Like them, he often
wrote it for special occasions and for
certain musicians.

When Duke's orchestra returned from Europe, Mills sent them on a tour of Texas. It was the first tour of that state by a black band.

The concerts given by Duke Ellington and his orchestra were very popular in Texas. However, racial discrimination in hotels and restaurants and by taxi drivers angered the musicians. Some of them said they would never again play in the South. Yet Irving Mills had already arranged another southern tour.

Duke was determined that his men should not be treated with disrespect. They would tour the South, but they would do it with dignity and in comfort.

When the band met at the railway station to begin the southern tour, the men learned that they were to travel in private railroad cars. There were two Pullmans and a 70-foot baggage car, each with the name of the band on its sides! The men would have their own food, water, electricity, and toilets. Their cars would be parked on tracks in the towns that they visited. They would not be dependent on anybody for anything.

In each city people came to stare at the private railroad cars. Often someone exclaimed, "That's the way the president of the United States travels!"

Duke had learned how to combat racial prejudice on band tours. However, some things happened that could not be conquered. In little more than two years, death took both his mother and his father. Duke became very depressed. Even his daily Bible reading failed to comfort him.

Something else bothered Duke. He was no longer happy with Irving Mills as his

agent and lyric writer. Mills had done him a great service, Duke realized, in getting the band good engagements. He had also helped with Duke's stage shows. Most important of all, Mills had scheduled many recording sessions for them. Records were the only means of preserving Duke Ellington's music. Written notes could not do it since each player had an individual style. Also the players sometimes added variations of their own at performances.

Yes, Duke Ellington owed much to Irving Mills. But lately Mills had become so busy and so successful that Duke and his orchestra no longer received his personal attention. So, in 1939, Duke ended his partnership with Irving Mills.

9. Duke Ellington, Composer

Duke's mood of depression did not last long. Before 1939 ended, he had a new agent, William Morris, and a new lyric writer, little Billy Strayhorn.

Billy was a pianist and composer as well as a lyricist. He traveled with the band on all its tours. Sometimes he took Duke's place at the piano. Like the rest of the musicians, Billy gave New York City as his home address, but a train was his real home for many years. Soon after joining Duke, Billy Strayhorn composed

"Take the A-Train." This became the band's new theme song.

Duke loved trains. "Folks can't rush you until you get off," he explained. "I love everything about a train."

The motion of a train and the sound of its wheels and its whistle often inspired Duke Ellington to compose. Sometimes the music came out a direct sound picture of train travel, as in "Lightnin'" and "Daybreak Express." More often, the soothing rhythm of the train merely stimulated his imagination. Then he would create something entirely different from what his ears heard.

One night Duke and his band were on a train traveling through Ohio. Billy Strayhorn was sleeping, and Lawrence Brown was reading. Harry Carney, Sonny Greer, and Johnny Hodges were playing cards. Other musicians sat looking through the windows at the bright towns that flashed past and the long stretches of dark landscape in between. They talked about music, about the concert they had just completed. They talked about the next concert ahead and about their troubles with their instruments. In the midst of the chatter, Duke Ellington worked on his new composition, "New World A-Comin'."

Suddenly Duke sang aloud a phrase of his new piece. "Da, da, da, dee, DO!"

Up and down the aisle, conversation came to a stop. Ears were pricked up to listen. The men nodded contentedly to one another. The new piece was going well.

When it was time to get off the train, the composition was ready to be tried out.

Although Duke Ellington liked writing

music on trains, he could compose in any circumstances. And he could compose at any time of day or night. He wrote in taxis, in buses, and in cars. He wrote wherever he happened to be when an idea struck him. If he had no music paper with him, he wrote on scraps of paper or on paper bags. He even jotted down his musical ideas on menus in cafés.

One night the band had to travel by bus from one engagement to another. Duke had promised a new piece for the next day's concert, but he had not yet written it. So all night long, in the dark bus, Duke Ellington wrote music. His musicians held lighted matches for him to see by. By the time morning came, several boxes of wooden matches had been used up, but Duke's new piece was ready.

Musical ideas came to Duke Ellington

from everything that went on around him. "Mood Indigo" was inspired by a poorly adjusted microphone in a recording studio. In fifteen minutes Duke made the sad whine into a slow blues melody, played by trumpet, trombone, clarinet, and rhythm section. At first Duke called it "Dreamy Blues." Later on the title was changed to "Mood Indigo."

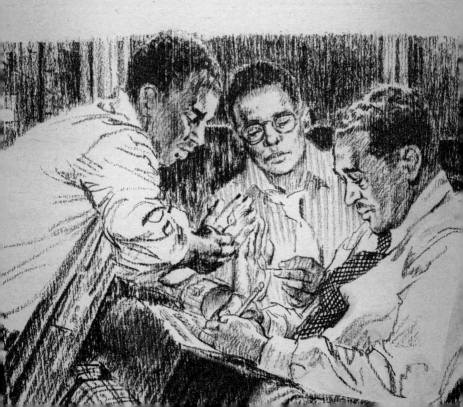

Lying in bed one summer night in New York City, Duke listened to the sounds of the city that came through the open window. He heard taxis clattering over manhole covers and tugboats whistling in the river. He heard the roar of the elevated trains and the occasional voices of late homecomers. Duke Ellington sat up in bed and scribbled down the outline of "Eerie Moan." Then he lay down again and went peacefully to sleep.

An air shaft, on which the bathroom window opened, inspired one of Duke Ellington's fastest, most explosive pieces. Duke heard his neighbors across the air shaft quarreling. He heard dogs barking below him and cats yowling upstairs. He heard people praying, fighting, snoring, dancing, laughing. All these he put into "Harlem Air Shaft."

One well-known piece was composed in the hall of a Chicago office building. When the band reported for a recording session there, they found that the studio was still in use. While standing in the hall, Duke Ellington held a sheet of music paper against a glass wall and scribbled some music on it. It was the basic pattern of "Solitude."

After a 20-minute wait, the band was admitted to the studio. Duke decided to record his new tune immediately. Coatless, wearing a pork-pie hat on the back of his head, he crouched over the piano. He played his new tune over and over, trying different variations.

The band members opened their instrument cases and began to warm up. An ear-splitting confusion of sound filled the room. Studio engineers sent frantic signals

to Duke Ellington to begin, but he ignored them.

Each musician took Duke's new theme and began to play variations on it. Duke kept on strumming the piano, but he listened to everything that his musicians played.

At last he stood up and yelled, "Quiet!"

Nobody paid any attention. Again Duke shouted for quiet. Gradually the noise stopped, and the rehearsal began.

From the piano, Duke Ellington worked out the details of his new composition. He gave one man a solo here, another there. In a very short time, Duke signaled the studio engineers that he was ready to begin recording "Solitude."

Later on the record won for him a $2,500 prize from the American Society of Composers, Authors, and Publishers.

10. King of Jazz

In October 1940, Cootie Williams took Duke Ellington aside. He told Duke that he had had an offer from Benny Goodman, one of the country's most popular band leaders. Goodman wanted to feature Cootie in his band.

Duke agreed that Cootie could not afford to turn down the offer. "Let me handle everything," he said. "Let me see how much I can get for you. You deserve to make some money."

"You'll have my job open when this contract is up?" Cootie asked.

"Your chair will always be open," Duke promised.

So Cootie Williams, after eleven years with Duke Ellington, left the band. Music critics predicted that without Cootie's trumpet, Duke Ellington's band would never sound the same. A composition entitled "When Cootie Left the Duke" was written by Raymond Scott, a band leader. It expressed the general feeling about Duke's loss.

However, Duke Ellington soon found someone to take Cootie's place. Perhaps the band did not sound the same, but it was as great as ever. Important as each individual player was to Duke, there was no one whom he could not replace. When a musician left him, Duke Ellington found another man he wanted. Each new addition to the band brought something fresh to it. Each became inspiration for Duke's composing. Yet the band never lost its distinctive sound, known far and wide as "The Ellington Effect."

Billy Strayhorn had made up that phrase. He said, "Duke plays the piano, but his real instrument is his band. Each member of his band is to him a distinctive color and set of emotions, which he mixes with others equally distinctive to produce a third thing, which I like to call 'The Ellington Effect.'"

Duke experimented constantly with different treatments of his pieces. In common with all jazz, Duke Ellington's music had strong beat. However, unlike much jazz, it also had rich melody and fine pattern.

As band leader, Duke Ellington was the anchor man for his musical organization.

Duke and lyric writer Billy Strayhorn look at some new music for the Ellington band.

His piano supplied the steady beat, the rhythm that kept the men together. As one of his musicians put it, Duke was "comfortable to play with." This is very important in a pianist.

Duke Ellington was also a great showman. He captured the sympathy and the affection of every audience with his appealing personality. Night after night he dance-stepped, smiling, across the stage.

Night after night Duke introduced one soloist after another to the audience:

"Harry Carney and his baritone sax!"

"Jimmy Hamilton and his clarinet!"

"Johnny Hodges and his saxophone!"

"Lawrence Brown and his trombone!"

The Ellington band traveled continuously, back and forth across the United States. They played a week here, a week there, or even a single night in city after city. They were on the go almost all the time.

The band performed in concert halls, dance halls, theaters, nightclubs, park bandstands, and hotels. They played in radio and television stations, in movie studios, and in recording studios. Everywhere they went, Duke Ellington and his orchestra were applauded enthusiastically.

During the early 1940s Duke Ellington

was awarded many honors. *Life* magazine listed him as one of the 20 most prominent blacks in the United States. *Swing* magazine chose seventeen of Ellington's 1940 recordings as the best records of the year. These included such pieces as his "Harlem Air Shaft," "Sophisticated Lady," "Concerto for Cootie," and "Never No Lament." (This is now known as "Don't Get Around Much Any More.") In a nationwide poll, 15,000 musicians selected Duke as the top jazzman of 1941.

11. *Black, Brown, and Beige*

In 1943 Duke Ellington celebrated the 20th anniversary of his move to New York City from Washington, D.C. New York and the nation celebrated with him. Newswriters named the week of January 16 to 23 "Duke Ellington Week." He received congratulations and best wishes from all over the world.

Duke Ellington had been invited to give a concert on January 23 at Carnegie Hall in New York City. This was a great honor, for the Carnegie concerts were almost always limited to classical music.

The concert opened with "Black and Tan Fantasy." Feet tapped all over the great hall in time with the music. Two pieces by Duke Ellington's son, Mercer, followed. Now 24, Mercer had studied at Julliard Conservatory of Music and had formed a band of his own.

Duke played several of his own well-known tunes. Then he announced a long, serious piece he had written especially for the day. This was *Black, Brown, and Beige*, a tone poem that tells the history of the black man in America. For years Duke Ellington had been studying the history of his people and collecting books on Afro-American life.

Before starting the new piece, Duke explained that the first part of *Black, Brown, and Beige* was built around old work songs and spirituals. "Brown"

described the different wars that black people took part in, and "Beige" pictured the blacks of today.

Duke finished his introduction and then turned to his band. People in the audience looked at one another, surprised. They had not expected serious music from Duke Ellington, King of Jazz.

With a great smash of sound, Sonny Greer introduced the slave songs on his timpani. Harry Carney's baritone saxophone came in with the melody. Other instruments followed.

Some people liked *Black, Brown, and Beige*, but others did not care for it. Listeners agreed on only one thing: It was too long. The composition, however, convinced Americans that Duke Ellington could write serious, complex music as well as popular songs.

During the intermission of the Carnegie Hall concert, Duke was called out on the stage. He was presented with a plaque that paid tribute to his contributions to music. The plaque was signed by 32 well-known musicians from every field of music.

As Duke accepted the plaque, he gave a large share of credit to his band.

Duke Ellington understood fully how important his orchestra was to him. It enabled him to hear immediately the music he wrote. It was also the medium through which his musical ideas were expressed.

Duke was able to express his ideas through his band because he knew his men so well and understood each one's capabilities fully. At the time of that first Carnegie concert in 1943, most of his musicians had been with him for more than ten years. Sonny Greer and Freddie Guy had been in the Ellington band the entire 20 years. Harry Carney and Tricky Sam Nanton had been with him for seventeen years, and Johnny Hodges and Juan Tizol fifteen. No wonder Duke Ellington could write a concerto for an individual player that fitted him perfectly and showed off his unique talents!

"Without my band," Duke Ellington once said, "I am of little value."

If this remark was true, the reverse was too. Musicians who left Duke Ellington's orchestra to join other bands usually discovered that they seldom had the chance of using their abilities to the fullest extent. It was not at all unusual for a musician to return to Duke after a long absence.

12. The Indestructible Duke

The busy years flew past. As Duke Ellington grew older, he gave up some of the things he had enjoyed during his youth. He had begun to worry about his health. He no longer ate huge meals. He stopped smoking and drinking, and he seldom went to parties.

Duke found a physician, Dr. Arthur Logan, in whom he had great faith. He consulted this doctor at the first sign of a cold or fever. Sometimes Dr. Logan was asked to fly across the country to give advice about a minor illness.

Duke Ellington himself had always refused to travel by airplane. He loved trains. Besides, he had little confidence in the ability of airplanes to stay aloft.

Late one evening Duke Ellington finished an engagement in Miami, Florida. Then he learned that he was expected in Hollywood, California, the very next day to work on a movie. The only possible way to get there in time was to fly.

Early in the morning Duke telephoned Dr. Logan in New York. He asked him to look out his window and see if it was clear enough for flying.

Dr. Logan rubbed his eyes to clear the sleep out of them. Then he put his head out of his apartment window. He assured Duke that it was a beautiful clear day. Of course, he had no idea what the weather was like in Miami!

Once in the air, Duke forgot his fears. Airplane travel delighted him. From that day on, he preferred planes to trains.

In most ways, however, Duke Ellington remained the same year after year. His elegance, grace, and charm remained unchanged by the passing of time. He was always calm, cheerful, and relaxed. He was never known to lose his temper, to say or do anything unkind. Every day he read his Bible and said his prayers. Almost every day he spent some time studying the history of Afro-Americans. He had collected more than 1,000 books on this subject.

From the 1940s to 1960s, Duke Ellington kept to the same full schedule he had followed in his younger days. With his band he made trips to Europe, the Middle East, the Orient, and Africa. He also went on many tours throughout the United States and Canada. In every corner of the world, Duke became a symbol of America.

Each tour inspired Duke to write more music. He wrote more and more long, serious pieces as time went on. In 1947 the African nation of Liberia asked him to write something for the 100th anniversary of its founding. After playing at the Shakespeare Festival in Stratford, Ontario, Duke wrote a Shakespeare suite. He called it *Such Sweet Thunder*. The *Virgin Islands Suite* followed a Caribbean trip. The *Far East Suite* was inspired by a tour of the Orient which was sponsored by the United States State Department. Duke Ellington wrote an opera, *Boola*, as well as the music for several shows.

In 1965 Duke Ellington again tried something new—a sacred jazz concert. He thought this was the most important thing he had ever done. "Now," he said, "I can say loudly and openly what I've been saying to myself on my knees."

His first sacred concert was held in Grace Cathedral in San Francisco. In the program notes, Duke said, "Every man prays in his own language, and there is no language that God does not understand."

So Duke Ellington and his band added churches and cathedrals to the long list of buildings in which they had performed.

Duke had largely given up "composing on the run." Most of his compositions were now written in the quiet of his hotel room or apartment. His music was carefully and fully written out. But there was still room for interpretation by individual band members.

"Jazz cannot be limited by definitions and rules," Duke often said. "If jazz means anything, it means freedom of expression."

After directing his own band for several years, Mercer Ellington joined his father as a trumpet player. About 1958 he became business manager of Duke's band.

More and more honors were heaped on Duke. He won an award from *Esquire* magazine as the leader of the best jazz organization in the world. Several universities, including Yale, gave him honorary degrees of Doctor of Music. The African Republic of Togo put out an entire series of stamps honoring musicians, and Duke Ellington was included.

Oddly enough, Duke received more publicity from a prize he did not get than from the many he received. In 1965 the

Pulitzer Prize music committee recommended that a special award be given to Duke Ellington for his long-term achievements in music. However, no prize was given that year for music.

If Duke Ellington was hurt by the slight, he never showed it. "Fate is being kind to me," he said with a smile. "Fate doesn't want me to be too famous too young." He was 65!

Occasionally black people complained that Duke Ellington took no part in protest marches or demonstrations for social equality. Duke marveled that his people did not understand him. All his life he had been trying, through his music, to help the world understand and appreciate Afro-Americans. For years his music had created a bond for understanding between the races and between the generations.

13. "Musician of Every Year"

One morning in 1966, Duke Ellington and his band gave a free concert for high school students in Seattle, Washington. A number of parents and a few grand-parents managed to get into the opera house too.

When the curtains parted to reveal the band, some people in the audience were disappointed. The musicians looked very, very bored. Could this be the famous Duke Ellington band?

Then Duke made his entrance. "All the kids in the band want you to know," he told the audience with his contagious smile, "that we DO love YOU. We love you madly!"

With a snappy dance-step, Duke Ellington moved over to the piano. He lifted his expressive hands, and the band came to life. They swung into "Mood Indigo," and the 3,000 students cheered wildly.

Parents and grandparents looked at one another with amazement. They had loved that Ellington tune in their own youth! Now it was popular with yet another generation of young people!

The same thing happened when the band played "Satin Doll," "Solitude," and "Take the A-Train." As usual at Ellington concerts, soloist after soloist was introduced. Among them was Cootie Williams, who had returned to the band after an absence of 22 years.

When the concert ended, three generations of fans jumped to their feet. They clapped and cheered for Duke Ellington and his ageless music.

April 29, 1969, was Duke Ellington's 70th birthday. Many celebrations were held in his honor. Ten nights in a row he

President Nixon awards the Medal of Freedom to Duke on his 70th birthday.

blew out 70 candles on birthday cakes. At last he said, "I've run out of breath!"

The most important birthday party was held at the White House. President Nixon gave a dinner party in Duke Ellington's honor. There were more than 140 guests.

As Duke was greeted at the presidential mansion, he must have thought of his father. Ed Ellington had served here as a butler. Now his son had come as a guest of honor.

Following the dinner, President Nixon sat down at the piano and played "Happy Birthday" to Duke. Then he presented him with the Presidential Medal of Freedom, the nation's highest civilian honor. This was the first time a black man had received it.

"This medal is presented to Edward Kennedy Ellington," President Nixon said, "for his exceptionally meritorious contribution. . . . In the royalty of American music, no man swings more or stands higher than the Duke."

In the fall of 1973, Duke Ellington made one of the greatest tours of his career. He played in all of the European capitals, and in Abyssinia and Zambia. Then he gave a "Command Performance" for England's Queen Elizabeth.

On May 24, 1974, at the age of 75, Duke Ellington died of cancer. However, his recordings keep his music alive, and his band continues to play it, with his son Mercer as band-leader.

For more than 50 years Duke Ellington had a strong influence on modern jazz. As one musician expressed it, "All the musicians in jazz should get together on one certain day and get down on their

America's King of Jazz, Duke Ellington, continued to thrill audiences with his exciting music until his death in 1974.

knees to thank Duke Ellington."

Nations around the globe are aware of the special debt today's music owes Duke Ellington. One example of this worldwide recognition was Duke's admission to the Royal Swedish Academy of Music. Duke was the first performer and composer of popular music who had ever been admitted to this well-known organization.

Perhaps Duke's contributions to music are best summed up in the words on a medal given to him in New York City in 1965:

Presented in appreciation to Edward Kennedy Ellington, known as Duke —"Musician of Every Year"—distinguished composer and worldwide Ambassador of Good Will...

Index

95

Hamilton, Jimmy, 72
Hardwicke, Otto, 13, 25, 32–
33, 36, 39, 42, 47
Harlem, 37, 38 (pic), 39, 40,
44, 51
"Harlem Air Shaft," 64, 73
Hodges, Johnny, 51, 60, 72,
79

Jazz, 25, 50, 70, 86, 92
Johnson, James P., 17–18, 21,
39
"Jubilee Stomp," 47

Kentucky Club, 45, 47, 49

"Lightnin'," 60

Miley, Bubber, 45–46, 47, 52
Mills, Irving, 49–51, 53, 55,
56, 58
"Mood Indigo," 63, 89
Morris, William, 59

Nanton, Tricky Sam, 79
"New World A-Comin'," 61
New York City, 26, 32, 36,
37, 42, 44, 53, 59, 64, 74,
81, 94
Nixon, Richard M., 90 (pic),
91–92

Poodle Dog Café, 20, 21
Pratt Institute of Applied
Arts, 26

Presidential Medal of Freedom, 91–92
Pulitzer Prize, 87

Ragtime, 13, 16, 17, 18, 19,
20, 25

"Saint Louis Blues," 49
"Satin Doll," 89
Snowden, Elmer, 43, 44
"Soda Fountain Rag," 19–21,
23
"Solitude," 65, 67, 89
"Sophisticated Lady," 73
Strayhorn, Billy, 59, 60, 70,
71 (pic)
Such Sweet Thunder, 83
Sweatman, Wilbur, 36, 39, 40

"Take the A-Train," 60, 89
Thompson, Edna, 13, 29. See
also Ellington, Edna
Tizol, Juan, 79
Togo, Republic of, 86

Virgin Islands Suite, 83

Waller, Fats, 39, 42
Washington, D.C., 10, 28, 36,
40, 41, 42, 43, 53, 74
"The Washingtonians," 25, 28,
31, 32, 34, 36, 39, 42, 43,
44, 45, 46
Whetsol, Arthur, 13, 15, 25,
26, 33, 36, 42, 45, 51
Williams, Cootie, 52, 68–69,
89